Flying High with Literacy 1

Also avaliable from The Questions Publishing Company Ltd:

Flying High with Literacy 2
Quality learning through a range of genres

Joy McCormick and Narinderjit Gill
ISBN: 1-84190-018-4

Flying High with Literacy 1

Quality teaching in literacy

Joy McCormick and Narinderjit Gill

The Questions Publishing Company Ltd
Birmingham
1999

First published in 1999
by The Questions Publishing Company Ltd
27 Frederick Street, Birmingham B1 3HH

© 1999 Joy McCormick and Narinderjit Gill

Selected pages in this book may be photocopied for use by the purchaser or in the purchasing institution only. Otherwise all rights are reserved and the text of this book may not be reprinted or reproduced or utilised in any form or by any electronic, mechanical or other means, now known or hereafter invented, including photocopying and recording, or in any information storage or retrieval system, without permission in writing from the publishers.

Designed by Al Stewart
Cover design by Lisa Martin
Illustrations by Martin Cater

ISBN: 1-84190-017-6

Contents

Acknowledgements	vi
Foreword	vii
Preface	ix
Introduction	xi
1 Using questions to develop learning	1
2 Children accessing research: How to make doing research interesting, lively and fun to do	4
3 Providing models for children: shared reading	7
4 Developing group work	10
5 Teaching the editing process: collaborative self review	18
6 Setting tasks with support	23
7 Pacing the work	31
8 The plenary	47

Acknowledgements

Our initial thanks must go to Mick Waters who motivated and inspired us to share and celebrate our work in classrooms. The practical examples on which this book is based could not have been carried out without the support of children and teachers in Sandwell LEA who were involved in the Quality Start Raising Standards Project.

We would also like to extend our thanks to:

- ▲ Grove Vale Primary and Leasowes Primary for providing us with children's work.
- ▲ Janice Wrigley who worked alongside teachers and developed the work at Grove Vale Primary.
- ▲ Wendy Bloom for her insightful advice on catering for children with Special Educational Needs.
- ▲ Jan Roman for her support during the final stages of publication.

And last, but not least, warm thanks to our families for their patience and support during all the long evenings, weekends and holidays that we spent working on the materials.

Foreword

The Quality Start – Raising Standards in Primary Schools – project has been one of the major contributors to raising achievement and improving the quality of teaching in Sandwell primary schools. The project, which provides in-service training, follow-up classroom support and resources, has enabled teachers to enhance pupils' learning of basic skills and to develop their own teaching methodology.

Improvements in teacher morale and motivation, in pupil response and achievement are evident across the borough. The project has also facilitated the celebration and sharing of good practice between schools and has demonstrated that there is a wealth of talent in Sandwell. The LEA was inspected in 1998 and Quality Start was highlighted for its significant impact on the quality of teaching.

Through the work of the project a range of teacher support materials have been developed by project staff in partnership with schools. These form the basis of this series of publications, and are a testimony to the talented leaders in Sandwell schools. The project has been developed in partnership with the St Martin's College, Lancaster, and we thank them for their contribution to ensuring that our young children receive a quality start.

Stuart Gallacher
Chief Education Officer, Sandwell

Preface

Flying High with Literacy 1 and 2 stem from work developed during an innovative school improvement project which began in Sandwell LEA in the West Midlands in 1996 and will finish in April 2000. 'Quality Start' has involved all of the primary schools in the LEA, with teachers considering the quality of their own teaching and collaborating in pairs to plan and develop the ways they work with children. Inservice sessions and the support of seconded teachers to work alongside them in classrooms have enabled different teachers to develop their own practice and critically review strengths and areas for further development. Support from headteachers has resulted in ideas being adopted across the school in many instances and the production of whole school 'teaching and learning' policies.

Quality Start has been an exciting project, and throughout its five years has had to adapt to different educational and political initiatives. The most important of these has been the National Literacy Strategy, with its emphasis on both the content of the reading/writing curriculum and the ways in which this content should be taught. These books focus on the teaching of literacy and will enable teachers to consider different ways of working (the practical ideas we all need) but also the rationale which underpins the ideas (why these ideas are so powerful). Book One examines the notion of high quality teaching and learning in the literacy hour. Any element of the hour can be approached in different ways, and indeed this variation will be vital as children build up a history of hundreds of such hours – the excitement being reported in many classrooms currently could easily turn into a classroom ritual – and then the thinking will stop. So, for example, there are many ways of teaching plenaries which will create the conditions necessary for children to consider critically what they have achieved and what they have learnt. Book Two focuses on the teaching of writing, with its emphasis on the range of text types outlined in the National Literacy Strategy. Again a tremendous number of ideas are included, each of which can be developed in many different ways. Each book stands alone but they complement each other so that together there is advice and ideas for teaching which come to us directly from primary classrooms.

Joy and Narinder have been key figures in the development and success of Quality Start. Their creativity in considering classroom issues and developing practical ways of addressing them has been one of the features of the project. These two books contain the results of this work and primary teachers will find them extremely useful as they look to develop the ways in which they teach.

Tony Martin
The Educational Development Unit
St. Martin's College, Lancaster

Introduction

There has been much debate recently, and a huge amount of controversy, over the way that literacy should be taught. Very often the classroom teacher is caught up in the middle of all of this, and not quite sure about which way to jump.

The classroom provides an arena in which teachers may work together, against a backdrop of recent initiatives and changing attitudes within education, to discover how they can best deliver the core curriculum and increase the opportunities for children to succeed.

This book has emerged from the work done with children and teachers in classrooms on the Quality Start Project, in Sandwell in the West Midlands. Aimed at raising the achievement of children, the project set out to explore the techniques and strategies that could best enhance teaching and learning, and that would provoke teachers into thinking about why they teach the way they do. The materials we have subsequently developed aim to provide professional thinking that underpins the work done in classrooms to develop children's literacy skills. Extracts of planning and practice have been used to try to help you to interpret ideas more easily and smoothly into your own classrooms.

Part of this book is also about helping you as teachers to come to terms with what you already do, and to see the links with educational initiatives, like the National Literacy Strategy. However, we are also keen to point out that some essentials of good classroom teaching will always stay the same, and are often hidden inside the latest terminology or framework for working.

We have tried to pinpoint the essentials of quality teaching and learning – those things which are at the heart of teaching in the way we do. These are embedded in the contents of this book and demonstrated through lots of practical ideas that have been extensively trialled in the classroom, and have been proven to raise children's achievement.

These are quotes from some of the teachers we worked with on the project:

> *'The change in my teaching approach has directly affected the children's learning.'*
>
> *'I plan for more group work now, which is truly collaborative.'*
>
> *'[The children] are more able to discuss in their groups now and have a go.'*
>
> *' Some of [what we have worked on during the project] has made me concentrate more on what I'm trying to focus on: the teaching and learning outcomes.'*

The book begins with two tables: looking at effective learning and teaching within a literacy hour, and choosing your teaching style. These tables act as summaries of the ideas which we will go on to explore throughout the book. Each section of the book focuses on a teaching strategy, and offers activities and ideas that you can use in your own classroom.

Looking at effective learning and teaching within a Literacy Hour

Whole class shared text/word/sentence level work
Make clear to pupils what they are going to learn (direction).
Show or model a process (to enable independent work).
Have strategies for making sure all children are taking part (questioning).
Target individuals with particular questions.
Develop vocabulary, explain terminology (explanation).
Develop skills and learn new approaches to working with text (demonstration, initiating and guiding exploration).

Independent working (Group work)
Introduce new work/extend previous work (initiating/guiding exploration).
Work intensively with a group of pupils (guided read/write).
Encourage paired and independent work (investigating ideas).
Plan for some differentiation in activities/outcomes/resources.
Set clear targets: specify timing for groups and what they need to prepare for the plenary.
Make links to previous lessons/shared text.
Train pupils to:

- ▲ follow common rules for class, group and individual work;
- ▲ work independently, know where to access resources, what to do without asking for help, what to do if finished;
- ▲ develop group responsibilities and roles.

Monitor lesson for pace and children's motivation.

Plenary (whole class review)
Keep momentum going by having a clear idea of what you want to achieve.
Have strategies for reaching this part of the lesson in good time (e.g. telling children they have five minutes before the plenary to get ready).
Support pupils' reflection and identify important things to remember for next time (discussing, arguing, listening to and responding).
Challenge children.
Discuss ideas investigated.
Help pupils to generalise a rule from examples.
Sort out misconceptions or misunderstandings.
Evaluate lesson and summarise key facts.

Choosing your teaching style – some classroom implications

Teaching Strategies (Definitions)	National Literacy Strategy	National Numeracy Strategy
Direction: Telling children what the lesson is about, pointing out key teaching points, drawing attention to how work should be set out.	Shared writing: Talking through skills as you write, e.g. 'let's not forget to put our comma in.' Directing children to key focus of session.	For example, 'Today we are going to learn to add 4 to a number using a quick way.'
Demonstration: Showing used to illustrate and reinforce key teaching points.	How to form letters. When reading make a deliberate mistake, e.g. 'that can't be right, it doesn't make sense – let's go back and re-read it'.	How to label a graph, how to use a key on the calculator.
Modelling: Practical demonstration in context, giving children the skills by talking through the thought process.	Showing children how to complete a writing frame together in collaboration, and also how to use a writing frame independently.	Showing children how to find a pattern in a number grid; can children can find their own patterns in their own grids?
Explanation: To clarify, give meaning to or explain. Introduction of a concept or vocabulary, telling children and giving the reasons behind it.	When writing a letter to a friend it ends informally e.g. lots of love.	Explaining the language e.g. rotational symmetry means . . .
Questioning: To deepen and extend children's understanding, identify their misconceptions, and help them to reflect and refine methods. A way of assessing, a starting point for children that can be reflective; setting a problem or challenge.	What types of words will add more to our story? Can you think of better words? Interrogate text, ask children why they say things in particular ways.	Are there any other ways in which you could solve the problem? How else could your results be presented?
Initiating and guiding exploration: Draw children's attention to problems, intervening in children's work, setting hypotheses to test later, setting up ideas, helping children to take their ideas further.	Search for 'ed' words in the middle of word and end of word, generalise rules, e.g. when does 'ed' appear at the end of a word? what type of words does 'ed' join on to (e.g. end of verb to show action has happened). 'We think a haiku poem is . . .'	Sorting set of objects on your own, sorting to a tight parameter – two criteria.

Teaching Strategies (Definitions)	National Literacy Strategy	National Numeracy Strategy
Investigating ideas: Facilitating learning, mainly in group work, using own ideas for working independently.	Investigate 'ed' rule further using a different text – firming up generalisation to summarise during plenary. 'A haiku poem is . . .'	Think of your own criteria to sort a given set of objects.
Discussing, arguing and evaluating: In-built assessment; could form the basis of plenary, encouraging children to predict and to question. Using children's own ideas as a basis.	Discuss 'ed' words that don't fit – challenge children and show that there are exceptions to rules. Character – develop a theory of inference by children, e.g. 'What makes you think that? Is she really a nasty person or are there other circumstances?'	Which operation is needed to solve a problem?
Listening to and responding: Identify children not contributing, respond to by stimulating and extending children involved, identify and talk about common errors, monitoring.		

1
Using questions to develop learning

Asking questions is an important strategy for both teachers and children to use. However, as teachers we need to be able to understand *why* we ask questions and be aware of the range of different types of questions we can ask. We need to provide children with a good model for the types of questions they can use too. The table overleaf shows basic types of questions and gives some examples. An example lesson plan to help you encourage children to question is shown on page 3.

Why ask questions?	What to ask	Providing good examples
Literal	Ask questions about what they see happening.	
Hypothesis/predicting	Ask what might happen if…	What evidence is there in the text? Why do you think that? Tell me more… (looking at children's meta-cognition, probing, understanding).
Explaining, cause/effect	Think of a reason why something has happened.	Why did they say that/do that? What caused that? Read me the bit that says that…
Summarising, discussing	Use questions to draw a conclusion.	Drawing all the threads together. Completing the jigsaw. Characters – what they said/did.
Arguing a case/evaluating	Question if something is fair.	Should that have happened to the character? Was that right? (morals principles) Would you have done that? What would you think if it happened to you?
Checking	Ask if something is accurate.	Where is the information? Read the text, show me…
Sorting (at a basic level)	Question if something is appropriate.	Is it in line with content/genre? Does it fit? Is that a poetic word? Is that the best ending? Did you expect that? Could you see that coming? Can you trace it back?
Responding, extending, refining	Ask a question in response.	Probing author's intention – what and how is the writing wanting you to feel? What effect is the writer trying to produce?

Example Lesson Plan

Encouraging questions from children

Whole class work

Explain to the children that the bear you are holding is your friend and is called Question Bear. Ask the children to think in pairs why he may be called that. Tell them the reason is that he likes children to ask him questions and that the focus for the session will be to learn how to ask questions.

What is a question? When and why do we ask questions? Let the children chat with a friend. Help them to answer these two questions.

Ask the children some more very simple questions – 'What is your name?' Let them ask Question Bear some questions to find out more about him.

Introduce children to the language of questioning. Model a question using the different question beginnings to find out what is inside a box. Then let the children have a go and record their questions to analyse the quality of questions asked.

Class/group activities

Discuss why it is important to ask questions, e.g. to help us find out information that we do not know.
Show children a non-fiction book and explain the importance of asking the book a question to provide a focus for what they will be researching or finding out about. Once the children have decided on a question they want to ask, in pairs they can discuss what part of an information book helps us to find the answer.

Give group 1 and 2 a set of questions related to a non-fiction book. In their pairs ask them to highlight the keywords that will help them locate the answer to the question. Using the contents page and index of the non-fiction book they can find the answers, using key words from the questions to help them locate the information.

Give groups 3 and 4 a non-fiction book based on their topic. In their pairs ask them to ask three questions to the book. Groups exchange questions and answer them using the contents page and index of the book.

Plenary

Children in groups 3 and 4 analyse and say whether the answers to the questions were easy to find and also comment upon how good the questions were.

Follow-up work

Display a picture. Can children think of a question to ask? Display the questions. Now get the children to try to answer them. Use the questions and answers to make a non-fiction book.

2
Children accessing research
How to make doing research interesting, lively and fun to do

Doing research to gather information for writing is a key skill for children to learn. The table opposite gives some examples of ways you can help children to develop research skills and keep their interest. As with all the writing children do, it's important to be conscious that there is always a definite purpose and audience for research, and to make sure that children are aware of this. Whilst children are carrying out research they become very involved in the process and develop a sense of pride and ownership in their results. As teachers we need to be thinking about, and letting children know from the beginning of the research process, *who* they will share their work with and *how* they will do that effectively. Some good ways of sharing research might be: through assemblies, displays, presenting to parents, writing letters to key people or friends, and inviting visitors in to school.

Starting Points	Examples of Activities
Pictures	Questioning a picture/photograph/cartoon, with class teacher modelling and recording language of questioning. You could use a range of pictures and focus on key questions, e.g. what is happening? what do all the pictures have in common? think about . . .
Raising Questions	Making decisions about which questions to use. Suggesting questions, focusing on question words (who, what, where, when, why, how). KS1: Question bear – use him to help guess what's in the box. KS2: what's in the box? more directed, could accept only yes/no answers. With all children discuss why some questions are more effective than others.
Artefacts	Demonstrate process of devising questions about artefacts, by identifying the precise information children wish to know. Problem solving activity: collect a range of artefacts in a bag; ask children to piece together the jigsaw of objects by asking questions.
Books, Watching Television Listening to Tape	Setting questions before using books, TV or tape. Could focus on HOW, and WHY. Try scanning a range of books on a topic and then focusing questions. Think about doing it more than once with a different focus each time.
Events	Trips, fetes – children could research and organise these.
People *(visitors, other adults)*	Interviewing: children devising their own questions. Showing understanding of what makes a good question. Children can work collaboratively to plan questions, practise interview format to evaluate the relevance, and effectiveness of their questions. Children can rephrase questions to clarify what they are asking. They can also build on their previous questions to gain additional information.
Media	Newspapers, report writing. Interviewing. Children formulating questions.
Poem/Music Of Time/ Historical Novel	Feeling of a particular era, e.g. evacuees.
Hobbies	Demonstrate how questions and answers are used to elicit or provide information by asking children questions about pets. Children can then explore the technique by asking each other questions. Children could use prompt cards (who, what, why where, when, how).
Puppets	Asking a puppet questions to obtain information e.g. using a fox puppet to find out more about their natural habitat. You could use role play situation, but you need to have content knowledge for the variety of questions that children may ask.
Environment	Children need to be able to pose pertinent questions, to analyse and explore ideas, e.g. during a walk, on a trip to woodland, or in the school playground. Encourage as much discussion and interaction as possible so that children begin to ask questions in a natural conversational context.

Starting Points	Examples of Activities
CD ROM	Children devise questions and access text from computer to find answers.
Display Table, Interactive Displays	Provides a stimulus for children's curiosity and motivates them to ask questions. By having unusual items you can structure children's thinking by saying 'I wonder . . .?' You could also set challenges over the weeks.

For this to be successful you need to keep up your own interest in the topic – it's easy to stimulate children, but harder to maintain interest as adults when working with material written at the children's level. Try using your local library, where you can read around a topic at your own level.

3
Providing models for children: shared reading

Children need to understand what is involved in becoming an effective learner. In everyday life, if we are to travel about successfully in unknown territory, or reach a new destination, then a map is always helpful, if not essential. Providing a map, or model, for learning will help children to understand what is involved in the process of acquiring new skills or in reaching a learning objective.

We know it is good practice to share objectives with children at the start of a lesson, but do we always share the secret of how we are going to work towards them? This is where modelling comes in – although modelling a process for children does not necessarily have to be done at the start of a lesson, rather it can happen at stages along the route to clarify the learning or to review what has been learned.

During the shared reading experience, the teacher models intonation to achieve meaning, and verbalises thoughts or questions that help to interpret unknown text. As they listen and begin to join in, children acquire strategies, their own internal compass, for where to go next. Modelling is used to do a variety of things:

▲ to involve all children in a rich variety of text;
▲ to give real life substance to learning concepts and understanding;
▲ to provide a context for children to apply a skill independently;
▲ to give children a skill to manage their own learning.

Children need to experience print that is beyond their reach independently. This also provides them with a view of what they are working towards – showing them what is possible, rather than giving them something to aim for which is completely unobtainable. To many teachers, providing children with the right level of text that supports individual development is a dilemma.

How can modelling support the learning of all children?

S.E.N.
Sit children at the front of the class so that they have a clearer view and are less likely to be distracted. This will be less threatening and intimidating if you want them to be involved interactively, e.g. to 'come and show me'. You must try to maintain eye contact at all times. This will give you an opportunity to re-focus the children's attention, e.g. 'do you see that?' The proximity also allows the use of touch to prompt.

High ability
Target through differentiated questions to extend and challenge. Try to have clear outcomes which are targeted and expected. These expectations need to be made clear to all. Part of the demonstration could include brief attention to the more difficult features. Targets that children can meet can then be provided for their independent work.

A closer look at what should happen

There are certain questions which we need to ask ourselves when we plan any activity; especially when sharing any piece of text with the whole class:

What do I want children to be able to do?
How will I show this?
How will the activity help develop their learning?
What language do they need to be able to know?
How will they use what they have learned?
How can I ensure that what they understand stays clear?

Now, imagine that you have to prepare a shared reading session using the text to focus upon punctuation. How would you plan to model it?

Use the table on below to check against whether you gave any thought to these key considerations.

The Modelling Process

Key Features	**Example**	**Yes/No**
What skills do I want to teach?	Awareness of punctuation. Ability to locate types of punctuation within text and explain their usage.	
How will I behave in response to the text?	Reading is clear, phrased and fluent with appropriate expression.	
How will I develop skills and knowledge?	Look for missing punctuation. Suggest alternative ways of punctuating text. Explore and analyse text to decide upon correct punctuation.	
Is there any special vocabulary that I will need to use at certain times?	Check that children use correct terminology in their explanation of how sentences work to produce meaning for the reader.	
How will I know whether children have acquired these skills?	Children will be able to decide upon appropriate punctuation in editing a piece of their own writing.	
How can I support children further with the instructions and expectations I provide?	Make expectations clear about what we are to learn before the whole class shared read. Use cue cards for the different groups that may be targeted later in the plenary. Use examples of children's work in the explanation. Incorporate children's contributions in the modelling process.	

4
Developing group work

Working in groups to develop literacy is not a new idea. However, despite our familiarity with it, the quality of the work and the response of the children is still sometimes questioned.

According to the National Curriculum teachers have to provide children with the opportunities to 'communicate effectively in speech and writing and to listen with understanding' and moreover to 'enable them to be enthusiastic, responsive and knowledgeable readers' (DfEE Key Stages 1 and 2 of the National Curriculum).

Indeed the extent to which children become engaged or effective is often determined by the presence of the teacher. Once the teacher is no longer taking a direct part in their work, it is all too easy to find the following attitudes developing:

▲ no interest
▲ someone else always does the work
▲ lack of confidence
▲ too little time to finish something
▲ need to find out lots of information (queueing up behind the teacher)
▲ too difficult
▲ fear of the unknown
▲ fighting over resources

We need to get children to be sensible, independent members of a group who can take responsibility for their own learning.

Buying roller blades to travel around the classroom is not enough . . . despite the respect you might get from the children when negotiating the fast corners!

Sometimes we plan for lots of group activities, each one giving the children an opportunity to visit a new area to learn from, but then we forget to give them the passport! Look through the table on page 12 and consider whether you as a teacher ever think about and, more importantly, *do* something about the strategies mentioned.

Quote: "They work in groups all the time"
Fact: Children working individually at the same table.
Quote: "They know they can talk to each other"
Fact: Children hardly ever talk to each other and don't know how to.

Custom and practice, and the fact that we *should* know about things doesn't always let us into the secret of *how* we should do something. Seeing something happen once doesn't help our memory or recall of how it went either.

So how often do we provide children with explicit experiences which show them what effective learning looks like? Independent attitudes and effective ways of learning are not achieved without our support and guidance.

	Yes, I do this	I need to do more of this
Using a variety of approaches to appeal to the differences in preferred learning styles of children, e.g. computer, drawing or designing, group discussion, role play, personal projects, word games, problem solving, stories with musical links.		
Having a clear purpose to the activity, e.g. relating it to the real world of children, making it link to the rest of what they do (sometimes things outside the classroom).		
Limiting the amount of teacher led/directed activities.		
Giving children group roles to support the organisation and planning of work.		
Using child self-review - recognition of what they do can lead to higher self esteem.		
Giving adequate time for tasks - timed targets provide a good pace for work.		
Planning into the lesson opportunity for talking about individual responses to work.		
Teaching children the basics: ● research skills; ● strategies for learning; ● subject specific vocabulary.		
Giving 'supported' challenges - giving them the opportunity to be able to use what they know already.		
Helping children to overcome difficulties - making sure that they know: ● what to do if in difficulty; ● under what circumstances they need to seek help from teacher.		
Providing children with good quality resources and making sure they know the rules of how to get them.		

Steps towards getting group work going

Getting the right approach

Helping children become effective group members means getting them to be good at asking questions about the way they work:

▲ *what do I need to do in this task?*
▲ *how will I sort it out?*
▲ *what do I know already that can help me?*
▲ *what resources do I need?*
▲ *how might I work with others to help me?*
▲ *what happens when I get stuck?*
▲ *what happens if I finish early?*

Time spent at the start of a school year illustrating the behaviour expected, and then highlighting good behaviour regularly throughout the year will get children thinking automatically for themselves instead of relying on the teacher.

Getting children to check their own progress

Sometimes we are so concerned with the content of what we teach that the processes become hidden for children. This is a particular problem, especially when you consider that they need to understand and recognise the skills they have that will equip them for more extended work later on. So that children can better understand what is expected of them as learners we need to provide them with a framework that they can initially work to, to grasp the stages they need to go through in their learning.

Prompt sheets are an excellent way of doing this. Children can refer to a framework kept alongside their work, and write on it while planning. You can also keep the frameworks in sets and laminate them to use later in reviewing work. An example of a framework – a drafting checklist for writing information texts – is shown on page 14.

Drafting checklist – writing information texts

❖ Do you think the writing is enjoyable?

❖ Is there anything missing or inaccurate?

❖ Do you think it is too long or too short?

❖ Can anything be missed out?

❖ Can you think of any helpful words or expressions?

❖ Have you made headings?

❖ Have you worked out where the illustrations will be?

❖ Have you thought about the captions?

❖ Have you included all the main points from your notes?

❖ Are you pleased with your writing?

Then

❖ Read the writing to a friend.

❖ Listen to what they have to say.

❖ Have they got any good ideas to improve your writing?

Now

❖ Is there anything you want to add or change?

Using a planning framework to produce a non-fiction book or pamphlet

1. Introduce and discuss the purpose of having a planning sheet.

2. Model how to complete the sheet using children's ideas on the current topic. Note that this will require a lot of modelling over a period of time. Explain the kind of information needed for each section.

3. Discuss the way in which these children will be working. This could be either:

▲ children in groups working on different sections each to produce a group book or pamphlet;
▲ whole class working to produce one book or pamphlet with groups working on different sections.

Both ways require children within their group to assign roles and responsibilities. Emphasis needs to be placed upon the fact that each group is dependent on each other to produce the planning framework. On pages 16 and 17 you will find examples of planning sheets that you can photocopy for use in your own classroom.

Planning the layout

| Types of writing | Headings | Subheadings |

| Illustrations | Captions | Other ideas |

Group roles

Important/key words

Group planning sheet: An historical story

Where will the story be set?	What kind of response will it have from the reader?
How long ago did it take place?	Describe the characters.
	Who will write about it?

The main events:

1

2

3

4

5
Teaching the editing process: collaborative self review

In Chapter 4 we looked at ways of developing effective group work in the classroom. For some tasks – in particular the editing process – paired work is the best approach. The pairs which work best are self-selected friendships, which generally produce work with no wide differences in ability or level. For paired work to be effective, we need to train children in the skills of co-operation. (Use the checklist on page 20 as a reminder of ways of helping each other.)

Working on the editing process can lead to the following learning outcomes for children:

- ▲ greater awareness of the elements of successful writing;
- ▲ ability to formulate and articulate their own perceptions of each other's work.

To begin with, it is very important that you should model various aspects of the work, including:

- ▲ critical review of a piece of work - against given criteria;
- ▲ ways of showing improvements, i.e. insertion, grammatical correction, rewriting or rearranging sections of writing;
- ▲ attempts at spelling new words.

You could introduce the above by using a typed piece of writing produced by a child of a similar age and ability.

A general approach

First, make sure that the children are aware of the audience and purpose for the writing. Ask them to consider what they feel is a good piece of writing: e.g. what makes it so? Ask them to read each other's work and think of something good to say: e.g. what do you like about it? Then brainstorm the ways in which we can judge other pieces of work, and form a checklist. (A sample checklist appears on page 21.) Now return to the work. Can children find other reasons now why they like it? Help them to extend their initial thoughts about it. The photocopiable sheet on page 22 can be used as a recording sheet for children's comments.

The next stage is for you to talk through an approach in which the children look at a piece of work and improve it, through:

- ▲ changing words for more interesting ones
- ▲ inserting words for better meaning or more interesting phrases
- ▲ crossing out words to make it shorter
- ▲ rewriting sections which don't make sense or need a lot of work to make them better.

Ask the children to consider what could be changed in their work and then explain to their partner. Discuss the findings and remind children of how to work through the task. Then let the children have a go, with the support of their partner and you the teacher.

Ask them to read out a few changes and say in what ways the new version was better. Throughout, they should consider the ways in which they are helping each other and what enables them to do this successfully.

Ways of helping each other

❖ How well did you listen to each other?

❖ Did talking to each other help to improve your writing?

❖ Was anyone helpful with what they said about your writing?

❖ Did you agree with what they said? What happened if you didn't agree?

❖ Did you ignore any of other people's ideas? Why?

❖ What would you do differently next time?

Checking your writing

❖ Is the writing interesting?

❖ Has it got lots of description?

❖ Does it make you think of a picture?

❖ Is there too much writing?

❖ Does it have interesting words?

❖ Does it make sense?

❖ Has it got a good start, middle and end?

Flying High with Literacy 1

Things I would improve . . .

Things I like . . .

6
Setting tasks with support

When you set a group of children off on a task, it's a good idea to provide them with a task prompt card. (You'll find some examples of these on pages 25 and 26.) Each task card helps the children not only with how they might work as a group but also on where to look for further help.

They also suggest ways in which children can improve their writing and may give key vocabulary for the children to use. Prompts with a precise focus like this, and used as an ongoing feature of their work, will in time help children into the habit of checking for and using appropriate punctuation and grammar. Each task also has ideas for how the children's work may be developed so that they have a purpose for what they do. This can also help to refine their thinking and reflection, i.e. prompt them to consider further questions about their work or the possible application of what they have found out.

Children can be placed in mixed ability groups to support their reading, or, alternatively, you might try:

▲ recording the instructions on to tape or a series of 'language master' cards;
▲ asking the children themselves to devise symbols illustrate 'contents page' or 'group roles', and then use these on the task cards to support the reading process.

To begin

Start as a whole class. Use one task card to illustrate how the cards should be used, and explain to the children that the cards are written to support them in their work.

At various stages in this task you should recognise, talk about and praise good behaviour, such as:

▲ concentration;
▲ distribution of group roles;
▲ using support systems or resources;
▲ ability to talk about/present their work;
▲ when group differences have been resolved;
▲ moving from one piece of work to the next;
▲ ability to take directions from the task card.

Further tasks

Once they are used to the way the cards work, the children can be left to carry out tasks independently. As always, make sure that you have covered all of the vocabulary that children might encounter before leaving them to do independent work. Also, it's a good idea for children to engage in their own self review of how they are working by reference to a checklist at the preparation, planning, action and review stages. (A sample checklist is shown on page 28.)

In the plenary session at the end of certain lessons, whole group self review can be done using the checklist to see if the class has achieved any improvement.

TASK – Writing captions

You are going to be thinking about matching captions to photographs. Some of these photographs will be in your library books. We will be using your work for a quiz to use with the books.

1 Try to match your photographs with the captions. Look carefully at how the captions have been written. (*Think about how you can work as a group to sort this out.*)

2 Find the pictures without any captions. Try to think of a caption for each one.
(*Use your library books to help you find some information. Remember to use the contents page and the index.*)

3 Write down the captions you have thought about. (*Check for capital letters and full stops.*)

TASK – Using photographs

You will be using photographs to help you think of some questions to use in your research work. What you find out will be shared with the rest of the class.

1 Look at your photograph carefully. Write down what you know about the picture. (*Work as a group to do this.*)

2 Think of something about the picture that you don't know about or want to know more about. Write this down: I want to find out . . . or I want to ask . . . (*Think about how your group will work now.*)

3 Use your library books to find out your information. (*Remember to use the contents page and the index.*)

4 Think about how you will share your information with the rest of the class. (*Think about what each group member will do.*)

TASK – Using a poster

You will be using a poster to find out some information. You will use what you have found to write a report as part of a guidebook.

1 Look at the title on the poster. Discuss with a partner what you think it will be about.

2 Now think of 3 questions you would like to know the answers to. (*Record your questions on your note-taking grid.*)

3 Look at the poster and see if you can spot any key words that will help you find an answer.
(*You may want to compare your key words list with those of other people in your group.*)

4 Read the poster aloud to each other and make notes on the information you find using your note-taking grid. (*Remember you don't have to write in sentences.*)

5 Use your notes to write a short report for other people to read. (*Try reading it out to someone else to see if it's clearly written and interesting.*)

Note-taking grid

Question	Key words	Notes

Note-taking grid

How are we working?

Before we begin . . .	Why are we doing this? Who is it for? What will it end up like? How will we know if we are successful?
Planning . . .	What ideas do we have? What could each of us do to help? Who does what? How do we do it? When do we do it?
Getting on . . .	How are we doing for time? What do we need to check? Are we on task?
At the end . . .	What went well? Why did we have difficulties? What can we do better next time?

Working with Year 2 pupils:

Leasowes Primary, Sandwell

Time spent in looking at group roles and responsibilities is a very effective way of helping children to understand how they can contribute to group behaviour and learning. Group roles and responsibilities can be used across the curriculum as the example below will show.

The class teacher wanted to stimulate children to think about creative but safe ways of arranging their own PE apparatus. To this effect photographs of each piece of PE apparatus were taken. Children were then grouped and asked to think about the roles they would need. With the direction of the class teacher they agreed to the following roles.

Manager - somebody in charge;
Checker - somebody to check the safety of the apparatus;
Recorder - somebody to draw the plan of how the apparatus fits together;
Technician - somebody to use the plan to assemble the apparatus.

This is an extract from the class teacher's lesson plan, describing the process of allocating the roles:

'Using the four titles the children in year 1 discussed possible job descriptions using the pictures as clues. (The writing on the original cards was blanked out.) Children were asked to think of some simple sentences which could explain the 'job' or role of the person with that card. The teacher scribed these and they were added to the bottom [of each card], so the pupils had their own group role cards which they had contributed to.'

(The role cards which she used are shown on page 30.) The class teacher and the children agreed what the group roles and responsibility meant and came to a common understanding. For the first session the apparatus was photographed after the checker and technician had put it out. In their groups the children compared their plans to the photograph using the criteria of accuracy, safety and enjoyment. Once a month children choose a set of apparatus pictures and as a group plan their PE session.

Encourager

My job is to help everyone and make them feel useful.

Reporter

My job is to tell the other groups what we have done.

Manager

My job is to organise how we are going to do it and make sure everyone understands.

Recorder

My job is to write things down.

7
Pacing the work

Tasks and self-review, as discussed in the previous chapter, are enjoyed by children and seen as a challenge. Sometimes timed targets can be used in association with tasks, but these should be treated with caution at first. If a group task involves stretching the ability of children in the skills and knowledge it requires, then adding a time limitation can create unneccessary pressure and can interfere with establishing good social relationships within a group.

Initially, short bursts of activity planned into the lesson and timed to last between 3-5 minutes can keep children focused, and will also set the working agenda and instil a sense of 'rigour and pace'. This can best be tried with children working in pairs during whole class teaching time. As children improve, time can gradually be extended for different activities, and pairs can become groups of four. Working like this, however, is a part of general classroom life as much as of a literacy hour, and can be used as appropriate across the curriculum.

Agreeing ways of working

To help children to work well together, we need to illustrate what good working relationships look like. A certain amount of coaching will be needed to establish some basic groundrules.

Behaviour	How do we achieve this? Activities to try
Listening to each other, appreciating others' point of view.	Timed trials: one group member speaks about something they have read about. At the end of one minute other group members have to: 1 think of a question to ask; 2 think of something to add; 3 think of some positive comment.
Taking turns in the conversation.	Appoint a group watcher. The group then has to discuss a subject they have read about for 5 minutes. While they talk the watcher records how many times each member speaks. When the time is up the watcher reports back on how 'balanced' the discussion was. The watcher then changes and the group try to get more even scores. If there are persistent talkers in the group let them take time out as the watcher, to see how others do it!
Sharing the task or paper.	Making sure the paper is large enough and the size of the group or table is small enough for the children to work easily together. Practice by suggesting quick written activities to either the whole group or pairs, with different sizes of paper in the centre of the table. Ask the children to choose the most appropriate size of paper and position around the table to work within a given time limit. Award points for the reasons they give for their decisions. Extra points can be awarded if their ideas worked!
Not interrupting.	Establish an award system for the person who 'waited their turn patiently'. Children could design a certificate showing effective ways to stay patient, or times when you need to wait for others to finish.

Children themselves can put together lists which can be put on display as a class contract for behaviour during group activities. The example opposite is courtesy of **Year 6 pupils at Grove Vale Primary School in Sandwell**.

Children can come up with quite detailed lists! To start them off provide them with two or three ideas on a large sheet of paper, for debate within their group and then get them to agree or disagree with the statements. They can mark the paper with ticks or crosses to indicate whether they agree or disagree, or they may choose to substitute other words which they think are better.

> ## Rules for working together
>
> 1. Co-operate with each other.
> 2. Don't take a decision without listening to everyone.
> 3. Don't just depend on one person's idea.
> 4. Make sure everybody understands.
> 5. Take part in all conversations.
> 6. Listen carefully.
> 7. Don't interrupt.
> 8. Share all the work.
> 9. Take responsibility.
> 10. Listen to the teacher's instructions.
> 11. Think of your own ideas.
> 12. Try your best for yourself / teacher / group.
> 13. Don't play with resources when someone is speaking.
> 14. Don't argue (vote or discuss instead).
> 15. Include all members of the group.
> 16. Show good manners.

Encourage each group to report back to the whole class, and then discuss their ideas. They can then add two more statements to the list and pass their sheet on to the next group. Discuss the ideas as before except this time, ask them not to substitute words but get the groups to give a counter argument on the bottom of the sheet, or to agree by providing further details. Pass the sheets back to the original groups. After a while children will have quite a few ideas about what they would like to include on a class list of rules. To begin with, get them to contribute other people's ideas that they thought were good rather than their own.

Getting children talking

Through talking with each other children can share experiences and consider what they know and understand. Discussion with a partner helps the learning along and is the foundation of successful group work later on. Short bursts of discussion time need to be planned into the lesson, so that you can best provide opportunities for purposeful talk.
Over the course of a week, consider how much time you dedicate to the following strategies (some examples have been provided for you to try).

▲ Discussion of a task and how to tackle it, e.g. sorting out a display of non-fiction materials/books in the classroom.

▲ Review of a piece of work, e.g. assessing whether a non-fiction book is still valid or useful for research purposes.

▲ Making predictions/suggestions, e.g. thinking about the contents page and what might be found under the headings.

▲ Observations – comparison, patterns/relationships, e.g. looking for words with the same root, linking key words to search for information.

▲ Reporting upon an event or task, e.g. children visiting other groups to explain to others how they did something, or to find out what others did, and then reporting back to their own group.

▲ Sharing and debating points of view, e.g. role play using historical characters, looking at letters containing opposing views before reaching a decision.

▲ Considering a statement, e.g. using the key words from the statement to research whether it is true or false, fact or opinion.

▲ Thinking about what we know already, e.g. thinking about 3 things we learned in the lesson yesterday, the day before, last week.

▲ Giving/receiving instructions/guidance, e.g. children who are 'experts' to support others using a programme on the computer.

▲ Sharing responses/results, e.g. children record their work on sheets of paper which are passed around the class or group for discussion, or using a 'jigsaw' technique – where one group of children splits up and takes on the roles of different specialists who, after working with other specialists have to return to their original group and report back what they have found or know.

▲ Explaining the process to others, e.g. talking about how a piece of non-fiction writing is structured, thinking through how to use the 'signposts' (headings, subheadings, captions etc.) in non-fiction to find your information.

▲ Reading partners, e.g. reading and re-reading a paragraph and explaining the main points to each other.

▲ Word processing, e.g. editing a piece of writing to include headings, subheadings or paragraphs.

▲ Writing partners, e.g. sharing the role of scribe when making notes from a book and translating these into sentences later; a partner can check for punctuation, or main and supporting ideas.

By being more aware of how talk is involved in learning, you may feel more able to ensure talk is being used to good effect in your classrooms. The following case study of a **Year 6 class at Leasowes Primary School, Sandwell**, gives some more examples.

A case study of one school's approach to how talk can be planned for and used for different purposes

A summary of working at Leasowes Primary, Sandwell, with Year 6 to develop speaking and listening using the language of persuasion

Session one

Discussion of issue raised: litter in the local area. A walk around the local area with a camera to take photographs to use as evidence for letters that can be written to local council focussing upon persuasive arguments. The aim of the letters would be to persuade the local council to help with the clean-up. Look as a class at photos taken and list the hazards to help with the content of their letter.

Model format for the letter and use of a thesaurus to find better words to persuade. Content of letter should be modelled a section at a time allowing children the chance to share their ideas and structure their thoughts.
Discuss to whom letter can be sent – children research possibilities. Send letters with photographs as evidence to Head of Waste Management services. (Examples of the letters are reproduced on pages 38 – 43.)

Session two

Brainstorm in pairs possible questions that could be asked if interview took place.

Task 1:
Questions recorded on board. Children look at questions and decide if they are open/closed questions. Explain to children what we mean by an open and closed question and model using questions brainstormed.

Task 2:
Discuss with children the sort of responses we may have to the questions and analyse in pairs whether this is the type of response we are looking for.

Children will need to be reminded of the purpose for the questions and what they hope to achieve from a possible interview.

Task 3:
Children have 2 minutes to decide upon the questions they would like to include and those no longer appropriate because not relevant or too closed.

(Our list of possible questions is shown on page 44.)

Session three

Children need to underline key words in question that they feel need to be stressed because of their importance. Model for children with: '**We** would like to take this opportunity to **welcome you** to Leasowes Primary'. Please note that this will need a lot of modelling before children understand the importance of the words which they need to be emphasizing. Children in pairs to practise saying the questions placing emphasis where necessary, adding intonation and pausing appropriately. Children will have to decide upon their roles: interviewer or interviewee.

Stop after 5 mins to look at one pair and see how they are working, and to reinforce importance of active listening. Do children have any general comments, e.g. type of question/response?
Video one pair for whole class to watch later.

Whole class – watch video – no talking. In groups of 4 children discuss 3 good points about the video and 3 possible improvements. Direct children towards thinking about:

▲ were questions worded to avoid yes/no responses?
▲ did questions lead interview towards required information?
▲ were questions rephrased to clarify information to ensure meaning has been captured?
▲ were previous questions elaborated on to gain more information?
▲ did some of the questions provide ideas for follow-up questions?

(Our lists of good points and improvements are shown on pages 45 and 46.) Children then have another 5 mins in their groups to discuss these points and add further thoughts to their original comments. Criteria for good interviewing developed by children. Questions refined in light of what practice interview highlighted.

The Head of Waste Management came to school and children had an open forum where they were able to ask their questions and have a real purpose for all the work that had been carried out.

Leasowes Primary School
Head Teacher: Mr. J.S. Atwal

Nine Leasowes, Smethwick, Sandwell, B66 IJA.

Telephone: 0121-558 1650

My Ref:

Your Ref:

MR. K. Cooper
Environment + Development
Services
Waste Management
Coney Gree Road

Leasowes Primary School
Nine Leasowes
Smethwick
Sandwell
B66 1JA
27/3/98

Dear MR. Cooper,

I am writing to inform you about the disturbing rubbish outside our school.

We have got a very severe problem that needs to have something done about it as soon as possible.

For instance there are 3 drains with no covers on them. They are deep dangerous and very threatening. There are planks of wood with sharp nails sticking out of them. If any one trips over they could catch themselves on them and could cause serius damage.

Someone could fall on the broken bottles and glass in the road, and as for the hole in the railway fence well, what can I say?

There are also bricks in the road which could cause a serius accident let a lone all of the litter like Macdonalds wrappers and beer cans.

It's not just polluting us it is damaging our natures health.

I have to point these matters out quite forcibly. Please help us.

We need your co-operation.

Please take a good look at the photographs.

Come and visit us at Leasowes J2

Yours Sincerely
Faye Sweeney J2.

Leasowes Primary School
Head Teacher: Mr. J.S. Atwal
Nine Leasowes, Smethwick, Sandwell, B66 IJA.
Telephone: 0121-558 1650

My Ref:

Your Ref:

Mr. K. Cooper
Environment + Development
Services
Waste Management
Coneygree Road

Leasows Primary School
Nine Leasows
Smethwick
B66 IJA
27th March 1998.

Dear Mr. Cooper,
    We would like to draw your attention to the mess outside our school.
    Our first problem is health hazards. For instance there are matresses that are not very nice to look at. There are carpets that are also rotting and black bags full of rubbish. All these things are possibly rat infested. This is disgusting to think about and something should be done about it.
    We also have a seconed problem. The second problem is also unpleasant to look at and think about. There are two or three drain covers missing and the drains are big, deep and dangerous. A nursery child could dissappear down one.

recycled paper

Another threatening thing is the hole in the railway fence. There are also gas bottles, broken glass which a little child could pick up. Theres also planks of wood and sharp metal on the ground.

I'm sorry to say but we have another problem. The problem we have this time is rubble. There are sacks full of builder's rubble which little children could fall over and cut themsevels. The cuts could possibly get infected. Also there are bricks right in the middle of the road. Bricks that are in the middle of the road can cause a serious accident.

Another problem we have is just litter which is causing a slight smell. All over the place there are broken chairs, broken cots and beds, metal, buckets, toys and all sorts of empty wrappers. All these things are disgusting. I am very dissapointed that the rubbish has not been cleared up sooner. I hope that something will be done about it.

In conclusion you will see from the photographs enclosed that the mess is horrendous I'll be looking forward to hearing from you. Also if possible can you come and visit us please?

Yours Sincerely
Katie-1 Allhi.H

Leasowes Primary School
Head Teacher: Mr. J.S. Atwal

Nine Leasowes, Smethwick, Sandwell, B66 1JA.

Telephone: 0121-558 1650

My Ref:

Your Ref:

Mr K Copper
Environment and Development
Services
Waste Management
Coneygree Road

Leasowes Primary School
Nine Leasowes
Smethwick
Sandwell
B66 1ja

27th March 1998

Dear Mr Cooper

We are writing to tell you about the rubbish and the broken things that are hanging around Nine Leasowes.

We would like to tell you about the four problems outside our School.

We need your attention for our first serious problem.

Our first serious problem that we have is that there are three or four drains without covers that are seriously big, deep and dangerous for the little children in the Nursey and Infants because they could fall down and possibly die.

There are also gas bottles that are dangerous and the little children could pick them up and hurt themselves.

There is also a threatning hole in the railway fence.

Our second problem that we have is that there are

recycled paper

rotten matresses and carpets that could be possibly rat infested by now because they have been there for such a long time. There is also black bags of rubbish that have been dumped.

Our third problem is that there is builders rubble in sacks just dumped outside in the road full of bricks.

There are broken lavatories, doors, draws, cupboards, beds, cots, chairs, buckets and toys.

While we are on the subject of broken things there is loads of broken glass, plankes of wood with nail in, broken sharp metal on the ground and there is also bricks on the road.

I am afraid that there is one more problem that we haven't mentioned and that is that there is loads of litter everywhere like crisp packets, beer cans (bottles) from the pub. There are mcdonalds containers, broken lights hanging from trees, all kinds of rubbish stuck in the railway track, cans all in the road, and loads of old road signs thrown in the bushes.

We think this is disgraceful and just in case you want to know how bad it is we have sent you some photographs which will tell you that we are very upset that you haven't done anything about it by now.

In conclusion we would like to invite to our school to see if you have any comments about it and to have a chat with us.

Your Sincerely.
Natalie Deeming
Louise Taylor
Abdul Razzal

Possible questions for interview

- Have you seen the mess?

- What do you think about the dreadful mess outside our school?

- When were you aware of the rubbish?

- How did you feel when you saw the photos?

- Why has this mess been allowed to build up?

- What will happen to the mess?

- Who will help you clean up the mess? Is there a way in which we can help?

- How long will it take to clean up the mess?

- This mess is really hideous – can we rely on you to clean it up?

- When is it possible to clean up the mess?

- Where will you start from?

- What are you going to do about the dangerous drains without covers?

- What will you do to prevent the build up of the mess again?

- What will you do if it happens again?

Improvements

- ❖ Need to speak up
- ❖ No fidgeting
- ❖ Pay attention
- ❖ Need to respond physically - nod head
- ❖ Talk clearly
- ❖ Be more confident
- ❖ Speak slower
- ❖ Some of the questions need to be missed out, as they are repeated
- ❖ Relax
- ❖ Respect each other

Good points

- Expression

- Concentration/paid attention

- Loud and clear

- Changing voice

- No fiddling

- Listening

- Good questions: give you information you need; open questions

- Tone of voice

- Looking at each other

- Inflection

- Effort in voice

- Polite – courtesies of speaking and listening

- Natural

- Checking answer to ensure correct meaning by rephrasing the question

8
The Plenary

Lessons which have lots of different activities carrying on at the same time are the more difficult to draw to a close successfully, due to the volume of resources and the fact that different children finish at different rates. Teachers often endeavour to achieve a final ten minutes during which the class can reflect upon and re-affirm the key learning points. But too often things get lost in the rush and teachers become frustrated, impatient with the ability of children to 'sort themselves out', and the whole experience leaves both the teacher and the class with a sense of dissatisfaction.

Sometimes the plenary is viewed as a quick summing up or 'round the tables' response. This can lead to a lack of focus, so that children do not really see the value in thinking about what they have learned. You'll often find that they are more interested in the problem of who they might play football with at dinnertime!

It is not possible to speak to everyone at the end of a session, although some teachers feel the urge to do so. However, over the course of the week it is possible to involve everyone if groups are targeted in a very focused way each day. The following examples are ways in which this may be done.

Menu of activities

▲ Summarising working: children describe how they planned the layout of a page of non-fiction.

▲ Directing and re-affirming key learning points: ask for the main features they have included in writing a recipe and how each helps the reader.

▲ Key elements of knowledge: children explain the main differences between how the contents pages and the index help the reader to locate information.

▲ Analysing the way children have worked: children can consider how they have helped each other in the way they edited a piece of their writing; or you could ask them to nominate someone in the group who has worked really well and explain why.

▲ How work may be improved and consolidated: ask children to say what they like about their work, what was successful about what they did, or how they might change something.

▲ Teacher-led: groups can report back upon something they knew about already that they used in the lesson and something new they found out.

▲ Responding and listening to individual children: reading out the part they liked the best.

▲ Problem-solving: ask what they found difficult about their work and how they tried to solve it, asking for help from other members of the class.

▲ Setting challenges: can you think of 3 . . . that you have found?; . . . and 2 more?; can you spell . . .?; how quickly can you find . . .?

▲ Discussing ideas investigated: prompt children's responses to others' work, i.e. do we agree with the report that has been read out? Have we any examples of our own that we could add?

▲ Sort out misconceptions and misunderstandings: as an assessment as children read out or volunteer aspects of their work; have a 'question time' when children can raise further thoughts they have had during the lesson.

Have a go at choosing something from the menu to do with a different group each day. Once you have found confidence in that move on to two things for two groups each day.

Once you establish a pattern of what you are looking for, i.e.

what you want to achieve and with whom, it gets easier to plan for what can be done in the time allowed, and do it well.

However, there are still other things which can get in the way, some of which are within the teacher's control and others which will need whole school cooperation. Some of the main problems to watch out for are:

- ▲ the over-exuberant caretaker doing party tricks;
- ▲ dinner ladies chomping at the bit
- ▲ class assemblies too early or too long
- ▲ poor time-keeping
- ▲ sloppy/clueless managing of workspace(s)
- ▲ interruptions or messages.

As we said before, one person alone cannot save the literacy hour! It needs a team approach, and the key to all of this is setting and advertising the agenda of how we work with each other.

Developing literacy skills: some learning points to support the planning

▲ Developing research skills is a difficult area – children need more time to develop these skills than an hour in the library can provide. Planning needs to take account of opportunities to target and practise certain skills across the curriculum.

▲ Clear decisions need to be reached on progression of activities, i.e. use of grids, writing frames, etc.

▲ Teaching time needs to be split between whole class, group activities and paired work. Time to talk and think can then be planned into the structure of the lesson. Collaborative work can be an essential element of making sense of text.

▲ Teachers may need to develop their own prompt sheets/frames/grids to provide a scaffold for children to use. Children also need to be offered the challenge of planning their own activities. In allowing children more open-ended tasks we are giving them the opportunity to extend their learning and develop their own questions and ideas.

▲ Wherever the lesson – perhaps in the school library – the teacher needs to establish a focal teaching point. A portable OHP with a range of texts on acetates could then be used for shared reading or modelling purposes in the focused work.

▲ Displays need to reflect work in progress within the school so children can access information from a range of sources, but could also be used to highlight ongoing and completed research work.

▲ Assessment information can be gathered at many stages of the children's work: discussion, brainstorming, concept mapping, note-taking, text restructuring.

▲ Children need to understand the process of what they are doing – this also means working at a good pace, with an understanding of the quality and quantity of work that is required of them by certain deadlines and at certain stages of the reading/writing process.

Developing literacy skills – using the school library

Through our experiences of working in schools with teachers, we have observed a variety of good practice. We compiled the following list of examples to show the processes that we saw.

- ▲ Establishing a clear purpose for using the library, rather than seeing a library visit as as an isolated exercise. All work should link to ongoing topics.

- ▲ Getting children to raise suitable questions for enquiry. Providing range of stimuli, e.g. a 'what's in the box?' game, interrogation of photographs, exploring artefacts, etc.

- ▲ Locating information using subject guides (short burst activities in the use of these), providing prompt sheets to support children in developing approaches, and the use of KWL and QUAD grids to provide examples of how to structure a line of enquiry. Children can be encouraged to develop their own grids to support personal research. It is important that children learn to develop the above skills in the context of part of an actual investigative project.

- ▲ Adopting appropriate strategies, such as skimming, scanning, and close-reading.

- ▲ Interacting with what has been read – highlighting key vocabulary or phrases, underlining relevant text, discussing the structure of the text, exploring different genres, critical response to text and layout, summarising.

- ▲ Promotion of self checking strategies, including the use of dictionaries or glossaries.

- ▲ Using note-taking skills from single and a range of sources. Show how reference to date published is a check for relevant or outdated information.

- ▲ Extended periods of research can enable children to revisit and work with information, to restructure or re-present it to others.

- ▲ Arrangements can then be made for children to follow up their own lines of enquiry – perhaps using a library 'licence'.

Getting the climate right

Throughout the book we have talked about modelling and providing frameworks for children to learn. However, these alone are not enough. Everyone knows that to build safely you need some sort of scaffold - and that is what children need too: a climate in which they are not afraid to have a go for themselves, where mistakes are positively enjoyed as part of the learning process.

Taking the steps towards independence will always be a gradual process as children move through school. It is very much a building experience in which *what* is offered is equally as important as *how* it is offered. Achieving independence demands a consistent whole-school approach to continue and build upon the ways we work in classrooms. Failing to do this results in a poor climate in which children do not have the conditions to grow and develop, and so will always be dependent upon other people for support.